TABLE OF CONTENT:

About Author: Meet Your Client-Closing Comrade (aka The Guy Who's Been in the Trenches)....2

Introduction: Ditch the YouTube Tutorials, Your Client-Closing Cheat Sheet is Here!...8

1. Chapter 1: The Referral Revolution: Your Inner Circle is Your Secret Weapon...16
2. Chapter 2: Networking Nirvana: Where Connections Blossom and Clients Bloom...27

3. Chapter 3: Niche Down to Rise Up - Conquer Your Corner of the Marketing Universe...44
4. Chapter 4: Outreach Odyssey - Where Relationships Blossom and Inboxes Don't Burst into Flames...55
5. Chapter 5: The Price is Right (and Non-Negotiable!) - A Masterclass in Valuing Your Worth...66
6. Chapter 6: Show Up Like the Marketing Maestro You Are...77
7. Chapter 7: Seal the Deal (and Get Paid!) - Where Dreams Become Dollars...86
8. Bonus...103

About Author: Meet Your Client-Closing Comrade (aka The Guy Who's Been in the Trenches)

Alright, before we dive headfirst into the nitty-gritty of client-wrangling, allow me to introduce myself, your guide, confidante, and fellow warrior in the digital marketing arena. I'm Prabhanjay

Tiwari, the founder and director of Prow Media, a marketing agency that's been making waves (and closing clients!) in Lucknow and beyond.

Now, I'm not gonna bore you with a laundry list of achievements or try to impress you with fancy jargon. Instead, picture this: a guy who started with a laptop, a dream, and a healthy dose of optimism (okay, maybe a bit of naivety too!). Over the past three years, I've navigated the exhilarating highs and the soul-crushing lows of the marketing world. I've closed hundreds of clients, from local businesses to big-shot brands, and learned a thing or two about what it takes to succeed in this crazy game.

But here's the deal: I'm not some marketing guru with all the answers. In fact, I'm still learning, experimenting, and occasionally face planting along the way (hey, nobody's perfect!). What I *can* offer you is a genuine, no-BS perspective, sprinkled with a healthy dose of humor and a whole lot of empathy.

Think of me as that friend who's always got your back, the one who'll tell you straight when your marketing strategy needs a makeover (no sugarcoating here!). I'll share my wins, my fails, and the lessons I've learned along the way, all in the hope that it'll make your client-closing journey a little smoother and a lot more enjoyable.

Why You Should Listen to This Guy (aka Me)

- **I've Been There, Done That:** I've walked the walk, talked the talk, and stumbled through countless client pitches. I know the struggles, the frustrations, and the sheer terror of that first client meeting.

- **No Fluff, Just Stuff:** I'm allergic to BS and believe in keeping things real. This guide is packed with actionable strategies, not empty promises or "secret hacks."

- **Humor is My Coping Mechanism:** Let's face it, marketing can be stressful. I'll keep things light hearted with a healthy dose of humor because, hey, who doesn't love a good laugh?

- **Your Success is My Success:** I genuinely want to see you succeed. Consider this guide as my way of paying it forward and helping fellow marketers navigate this crazy world.

So, buckle up, my friend! We're about to embark on a client-closing adventure filled with laughter,

learning, and maybe even a few facepalms along the way. But hey, that's all part of the fun, right?

Introduction: Ditch the YouTube Tutorials, Your Client-Closing Cheat Sheet is Here!

Okay, fellow marketers, let's get real. We've all been there. Staring blankly at our screens, wondering how the heck to turn those "potential" clients into actual, paying ones. You've probably lost count of how many YouTube videos you've watched, promising the "secret formula" to closing deals. But let's face it, most of them are full of fluff and leave you feeling more confused than ever.

Well, my friend, consider this your official intervention. This isn't some generic, rehashed advice you'll find anywhere. It's a battle-tested, no-BS guide, forged in the trenches of real-world experience. I'm Prabhanjay, and I've spent the last 3+ years building my agency, Prow Media, from the ground up. I've faced the struggles, the rejections, and the moments of sheer panic wondering if I'd ever land a client. But guess what? I did. And so can you.

This guide is like grabbing a Coffee with your marketing mentor (that's me!), who's going to spill all the secrets, shortcuts, and hard-earned wisdom they wish they knew when starting out. No more empty promises, no more guru jargon, just straight-talking, actionable advice that actually works.

Consider me your partner in crime on this wild client-closing journey. I'm here to cheer you on, offer support, and help you navigate the minefield of landing those dream clients. Because let's be honest, building a successful agency is tough enough without having to decipher cryptic YouTube tutorials. I want to see you succeed, to bypass the roadblocks I encountered, and to build a thriving business that fuels your passion and fills your pockets.

As the legendary Zig Ziglar once said, "You can have everything in life you want if you will just help enough other people get what they want." That's my mission with this guide. To empower you, to equip you with the tools and knowledge you need to attract and close clients with confidence.

So, put on your comfy pajamas, grab your favorite beverage, and get ready to dive into the good stuff. By the time you finish this guide, you'll be armed with the knowledge, strategies, and confidence to close clients like a boss. No more endless proposals, no more ghosting clients, just a steady stream of exciting projects and happy customers.

Trust me! Closing clients won't be a mystery anymore
Finally crack the client-closing code? Let's do this together!

P.S. This guide is packed with real-life

examples, hilarious anecdotes, and maybe even a few embarrassing stories (hey, we all have them!). Consider this your friendly pep talk, your strategic playbook, and your permission slip to ditch the BS and embrace a client-closing journey that's both effective and enjoyable. Because let's face it, marketing should be fun, not a soul-crushing endeavor!

Chapter 1: The Referral Revolution: Your Inner Circle is Your Secret Weapon

Forget cold calls and generic emails for a moment. Your first wave of clients is likely hiding in plain sight – within your very own network! Think of it as your personal client goldmine, ripe for the taking. But how do you tap into this hidden treasure trove? Let's dive in:

1.1 Shout it From the Rooftops (or at Least Your Social Media)

Remember that time you aced that presentation, or baked that incredible cake, and everyone couldn't stop singing your praises? Well, it's time to channel that same energy into promoting your agency.

"The best advertising does not feel like advertising." - Tom Fishburne

Don't be shy about letting your friends, family, former colleagues, and even your friendly neighborhood chai wala know that you've launched a kickass marketing agency. Talk about it with passion, enthusiasm, and a sprinkle of confidence.

Think beyond just casual conversations. Leverage the power of social media! Announce your agency launch with a bang. Craft a compelling story, share your vision, and highlight your services. Encourage your connections to share your post, spread the word, and become your brand ambassadors.

1.2 Content that Makes Them Say "Wow!"

"Content is king, but marketing is queen and runs the household." - Gary Vaynerchuk

In the digital age, content is your currency. Create valuable, shareable content that showcases your expertise and positions you as a thought leader in your field. Think insightful blog posts, engaging videos, eye-catching infographics, and maybe even a hilarious meme or two.

Remember, your content should not only educate and entertain but also inspire action. Encourage your audience to share your content, tag their friends, and spread the word about your agency.

Pro Tip: Don't just create content for the sake of it. Focus on quality over quantity. Think about the challenges your target audience faces and create content that provides solutions and adds value to their lives.

1.3 The Power of "Word-of-Mouth" Marketing 2.0

"The purpose of business is to create a

catchy headlines, and clear calls to action.

- **Incentivize Sharing:** Consider offering referral bonuses or discounts to those who recommend your services.

- **Engage with Your Audience:** Respond to comments, answer questions, and foster a sense of community around your brand.

1.4 Embrace the Awkward (Yes, Really!)

"To be yourself in a world that is constantly trying to make you something

customer who creates customers." - Shiv Singh

Word-of-mouth marketing has always been a powerful tool, and in the digital age, it's even more potent. When someone you know recommends your services, it comes with a built-in layer of trust and credibility.

So, how do you amplify this "word-of-mouth" magic?

- **Make it Easy to Share:** Create content that's easily shareable across different platforms. Use compelling visuals, *else is the greatest accomplishment." - Ralph Waldo Emerson*

Let's be honest, self-promotion can feel awkward, especially for us introverted folks. But here's the thing: if you don't believe in your agency and its value, how can you expect others to?

Embrace the awkwardness, step out of your comfort zone, and let your passion shine through. Talk about your services with confidence, highlight your unique selling points, and don't be afraid to toot your own horn (within reason, of course!).

Pro Tip: Practice your "elevator pitch." Be able to concisely and compellingly explain what your agency does and how it benefits clients.

1.5 The Referral Ripple Effect

Think of referrals as a pebble dropped in a pond. The initial impact might seem small, but the ripples spread far and wide. Each referral has the potential to generate more referrals, creating a powerful chain reaction that can significantly boost your client base.

Key Takeaways:

- Your network is your first and most valuable source of clients.
- Create high-quality, shareable content that showcases your expertise.
- Encourage your network to spread the word about your agency.
- Embrace the art of self-promotion and communicate your value with confidence.
- Leverage the power of "word-of-mouth" marketing 2.0 to amplify your reach.

By tapping into the power of referrals, you'll not only land your first clients but also build a solid foundation for long-term success. So, go forth and unleash the referral revolution!

Chapter 2: Networking Nirvana: Where Connections Blossom and Clients Bloom

"Networking is not about just connecting people. It's about connecting people with people, people with ideas, and people with opportunities." - Michele Jennae

Alright, let's talk about networking, shall we? Now, before you roll your eyes and conjure up images of awkward handshakes and forced small talk at stuffy industry events, let me assure you: this is a different kind of networking. This is about building genuine connections, fostering meaningful relationships, and creating a network that not only supports your growth but also showers you with client referrals.

Think of your network as a vibrant garden. Each connection is a seed with the potential to blossom into a beautiful flower (or in our case, a lucrative client!). But just like any garden, it needs nurturing, care, and the right environment to thrive.

1. Quality Over Quantity: Ditch the "Connection Hoarding" Mentality

Let's be honest, we've all been guilty of it at some point – that insatiable urge to amass LinkedIn connections like they're trophies. But here's the truth: a bloated network filled with random strangers is about as useful as a screen door on a submarine.

- Instead of focusing on sheer numbers, prioritize quality connections. Seek out individuals who align with your niche, share your values, and can genuinely benefit from your services (and vice versa). Remember, it's not about who you know, it's about who *knows* you and values what you bring to the table.

- **The Power of the "Why":** When reaching out, clearly articulate why you want to connect and how both parties can benefit from the relationship. Are you impressed by their work? Do you share common interests? Let them know!

- **Engage and Elevate:** Don't just connect and disappear. Engage with their content, participate in relevant discussions, and offer valuable insights. Remember, networking is a two-way street.

Beyond the Blue Platform: Exploring Other Avenues

While LinkedIn is a powerful tool, don't limit yourself to the digital realm. Attend industry events, join local business groups, and participate in workshops or conferences. Face-to-face interactions can forge deeper connections and create lasting impressions.

2. The Art of the Follow-Up: Nurturing the Seeds of Connection

"The fortune is in the follow-up." - Jim Rohn

Building a network isn't a one-and-done activity. It requires consistent effort and nurturing. After connecting with someone, follow up with a thoughtful message, share relevant articles, or invite them for a virtual coffee chat. Keep the conversation flowing and build rapport over time.

In the digital age, first impressions matter more than ever. When reaching out to potential connections, ditch the generic "I'd like to add you to my professional network" message. Instead, craft personalized messages that demonstrate genuine interest and highlight the value you offer.

Here are a few tips to make your introductions stand out:

- **Do your research:** Take a few minutes to browse their profile, understand their work, and identify common interests or areas of collaboration.

- **Compliment their work:** Everyone loves a genuine compliment. Acknowledge their achievements, highlight something specific you admire about their work, and show them you're not just another random connection request.

- **Offer value upfront:** Instead of immediately pitching your services, offer something valuable – a helpful resource, an insightful article, or an invitation to a relevant webinar. This demonstrates your expertise and builds goodwill.

- **Keep it concise and engaging:** No one wants to read a novel in their inbox. Keep your messages short, sweet, and to the point.

3. From Connection to Conversation: Nurturing Relationships that Last

Building a strong network isn't a one-and-done deal. It requires consistent effort, genuine engagement, and a willingness to nurture relationships over time.

Here's how to keep those connections blooming:

- **Engage with their content:** Like, comment, and share their posts. Show genuine interest in their work and contribute to the conversation.

- **Offer support and encouragement:** Celebrate their successes, offer words of encouragement during challenges, and be a supportive presence in their professional journey.

- **Connect offline:** Whenever possible, take the relationship offline. Grab a coffee, attend industry events together, or schedule virtual meetings to deepen the connection.

- **Be a giver, not just a taker:** Networking is a two-way street. Look for opportunities to help your connections, offer valuable advice, and connect them with others in your network.

4. Navigating the Networking Minefield: Beware of Client Thieves

"Keep your friends close, and your clients closer." - (Okay, I just made that up, but it's true!)

While networking can be a powerful tool for client acquisition, it's important to be aware of the potential pitfalls. Not everyone in your network has your best interests at heart. Some might see you as a competitor or even try to poach your clients.

Here's how to protect yourself:

- **Be selective with your connections:** Don't connect with just anyone. Be discerning and prioritize those who align with your values and business goals.

- **Don't overshare:** While it's important to be open and authentic, be mindful of sharing sensitive information about your clients or business strategies.

- **Set clear boundaries:** If you sense someone is trying to take advantage of your network or steal your clients, don't hesitate to address the issue directly and set clear boundaries.

- **Build trust gradually:** Don't rush into sharing confidential information or referrals until you've established a strong foundation of trust with your connections.

5. Reaping the Rewards: Turning Connections into Clients

When done right, networking can be a goldmine for client acquisition. As you nurture your relationships and build a strong reputation, referrals will start flowing naturally.

Here are a few tips to maximize your networking efforts:

- **Be clear about your services:** Make sure your connections understand what you do and how you can help them.

- **Ask for referrals:** Don't be afraid to ask your connections for referrals if they know someone who could benefit from your services.

- **Stay top-of-mind:** Regularly engage with your network and share valuable content to keep yourself top-of-mind.

In Conclusion

Networking is an ongoing process that requires effort, authenticity, and a genuine desire to connect with others. By cultivating a strong network, you'll not only gain valuable support and insights but also unlock a steady stream of clients who are ready to work with you. So, ditch the "connection hoarding" mentality, embrace the art of personalized engagement, and watch your business flourish in the fertile ground of Networking Nirvana.

Key Takeaways:

- **Be strategic:** Focus on building relationships with the *right* people.
- **Be genuine:** Show genuine interest in others and their work.

- **Be consistent:** Nurture your network with regular engagement and follow-up.
- **Be protective:** Safeguard your clients and your business.
- **Be valuable:** Offer something unique and contribute to the community.

By mastering the art of networking, you'll create a powerful support system that fuels your agency's success. So go forth, connect, engage, and watch your client base flourish!

Chapter 3: Niche Down to Rise Up - Conquer Your Corner of the Marketing Universe

"You can't be everything to everyone." It's a cliché, sure, but in the cutthroat world of digital marketing, it's a truth bomb worth exploding.

It's like trying to catch every fish in the

ocean with a single hook – you'll end up with nothing but exhausted arms and an empty bucket.

Think about it: in a sea of agencies all vying for the same clients, how do you stand out? How do you become the undeniable choice, the go-to expert that clients can't resist? The Absolute answer is NO you can't.

Instead, embrace the power of niching down. Think of it as conquering your own little corner of the marketing universe. Become the undisputed ruler of that space, the go-to expert who knows the terrain inside and out.

Why Niching Down is Your Secret Weapon

- **Cut Through the Noise:** The digital marketing landscape is crowded, with agencies popping up faster than mushrooms after a rainstorm. Niching down helps you differentiate yourself from the sea of generalists and attract clients seeking specialized expertise.

- **Become an Authority:** When you focus on a specific niche, you can delve deep into its nuances, understand its challenges, and develop tailored solutions. This positions you as an authority in that area, making you the obvious choice for businesses seeking targeted expertise.

- **Attract Ideal Clients:** Instead of casting a wide net and hoping for the best, niching down allows you to attract clients who are a perfect fit for your services. This leads to stronger relationships, better results, and higher client satisfaction.

- **Streamline Your Marketing:** Knowing your niche inside and out makes it easier to tailor your marketing efforts and reach the right audience. You can speak their language, address their specific pain points, and offer solutions that resonate with their needs.

Beyond the Industry: Niching Down by Service

Niching down isn't just about choosing an industry; it's also about specializing in specific services. Are you a Facebook Ads wizard? A content marketing maestro? An SEO guru?

Here are some examples of service-based niches:

- **Social Media Advertising:** Focus on creating and managing highly targeted ad campaigns on platforms like Facebook, Instagram, and LinkedIn.

- **Content Marketing:** Specialize in crafting compelling content that attracts, engages, and converts audiences. This could include blog posts, articles, videos, infographics, and more.

- **Search Engine Optimization (SEO):** Help businesses improve their online visibility and organic search rankings through on-page optimization, link building, and keyword research.

- **Email Marketing:** Become an expert in creating effective email campaigns that nurture leads, drive sales, and build customer loyalty.

- **Website Design and Development:** Focus on creating user-friendly, high-converting websites that align with clients' brand identities and business goals.

The Untapped Niche Goldmine

Don't limit yourself to the obvious, high-paying niches. There's a whole world of untapped potential waiting to be discovered. Think about industries or services that are often overlooked or underserved by marketers.

Here are a few ideas to get your creative juices flowing:

- **Sustainable and Eco-Friendly Businesses:** Help businesses in the sustainability space reach their target audience and promote their eco-conscious products or services.
- **Local Businesses:** Become the marketing hero for local businesses in your community, helping them thrive in the digital age.

- **Non-Profits and NGOs:** Use your marketing skills to support organizations making a positive impact on the world.

- **Creative Professionals:** Offer specialized marketing services to artists, musicians, designers, and other creative individuals.

The Niche Navigator: Finding Your Sweet Spot

Choosing a niche is a personal journey. It's about finding the sweet spot where your passions, skills, and market demand intersect.

Here are some questions to guide your exploration:

- **What are you passionate about?** What industries or services genuinely excite you?
- **What are your strengths?** What marketing skills do you excel at?
- **Where is the demand?** Are there any underserved niches in the market?
- **What are your values?** Do you want to work with businesses that align with your personal values?

Remember: Niching down doesn't mean limiting your potential. It's about focusing your energy, honing your expertise, and becoming the undisputed champion of your chosen domain. So, embrace your inner specialist, conquer your corner of the marketing universe, and watch your client roster flourish!

"Become the expert in one thing, and you'll be the go-to person for everything related to it." - Someone wise (probably)

Chapter 4: Outreach Odyssey - Where Relationships Blossom and Inboxes Don't Burst into Flames

Alright, my friend, you've got your killer website, your niche is locked and loaded, and your social media game is strong.

Now, it's time to unleash the power of outreach and attract those dream clients. But hold on! Before you go blasting generic messages like a marketing machine gone rogue, let's dive into the art of meaningful engagement.

Forget the "Spray and Pray" Approach

Remember those annoying telemarketers who interrupt your dinner with robotic pitches and zero personalization? Yeah, don't be that marketer. Generic outreach messages are the digital equivalent of spam calls – they're annoying, ineffective, and often end up in the virtual trash bin (or worse, marked as spam!).

The Power of Personalized Connection

Instead of treating potential clients like faceless entities in a database, approach them as individuals with unique needs and challenges. Imagine you're meeting them at a networking event. You wouldn't just shove a business card in their face and shout, "Hire me!" You'd strike up a conversation, learn about their interests, and find common ground.

Think of it like this: "People don't care how much you know until they know how much you care." (Theodore Roosevelt). Show genuine interest in their business, offer valuable insights, and demonstrate your expertise without being overly promotional.

Apply the same principle to your outreach. Research their business, understand their pain points, and tailor your message accordingly. Here are a few ways to personalize your outreach:

- **Highlight a Specific Challenge:** "Hi [Name], I noticed your website isn't optimized for mobile devices. This could be costing you valuable leads..."

- **Offer a Genuine Compliment:** "Hi [Name], I was impressed by your recent blog post on [topic]. It's clear you're passionate about [industry]..."

- **Share a Relevant Resource:** "Hi [Name], I came across this article on [relevant topic] and thought it might be helpful for your business..."

The Value-Packed Approach

Instead of bombarding potential clients with self-promotional messages, focus on providing value upfront. Offer helpful insights, share relevant resources, and demonstrate your expertise without the hard sell. This positions you as a trusted advisor, not just another salesperson.

Building a Portfolio (Even if it Means Working for Free)

In the beginning, building a portfolio can feel like a catch-22. Clients want to see your work, but you need clients to create work. So, what's a budding marketer to do? Consider offering your services for free or at a discounted rate to a select few clients.

This allows you to:

- **Gain valuable experience:** Real-world projects are the best way to hone your skills and build confidence.

- **Showcase your capabilities:** A strong portfolio is a powerful tool for attracting paying clients.

- **Build relationships:** Even if you're working for free, treat these clients with the same level of professionalism and dedication as you would paying clients. You never know what future opportunities might arise.

The Long Game of Outreach

"The best marketing doesn't feel like marketing." (Tom Fishburne)

Outreach isn't a sprint; it's a marathon. Don't expect to close every client with your first message. It's about building relationships, nurturing leads, and staying top-of-mind.

Here are a few tips for playing the long game:

- **Follow Up (Without Being Annoying):** Send a follow-up message a few days after your initial outreach. Keep it brief, reiterate your value proposition, and offer to answer any questions.

- **Provide Consistent Value:** Share valuable content, engage with their social media posts, and offer helpful insights on a regular basis.

- **Be Patient:** Building trust takes time. Don't get discouraged if you don't see immediate results. Keep nurturing those relationships, and the clients will come.

Outreach is an adventure, not a chore. Embrace the journey, connect with potential clients on a human level, and watch your client roster grow.

Key Takeaways:

- **Personalization is paramount:** Tailor your outreach messages to each individual client, demonstrating genuine interest and understanding.

- **Build a portfolio strategically:** Offer free services to gain experience and showcase your skills.

- **Play the long game:** Focus on building relationships and nurturing leads.

- **Provide value upfront:** Offer valuable insights and demonstrate your expertise without being overly promotional.

By mastering the art of outreach, you'll transform your inbox from a barren wasteland into a thriving hub of client connections. So go forth, my friend, and conquer the outreach odyssey!

Chapter 5: The Price is Right (and Non-Negotiable!) - A Masterclass in Valuing Your Worth

Alright, my friend, let's talk about the elephant in the room: money.
Specifically, how to confidently price your services and avoid the dreaded discount dance that leaves you feeling undervalued and underpaid.

Here's the truth: you are not a discount bin find. You're a skilled digital marketer with valuable expertise to offer. Your time, your knowledge, your creative genius – it all has a price tag, and it's time to own that.

Think of it this way: you're not just selling marketing services, you're selling your time, your expertise, and your creative genius. You're a problem-solver, a strategist, and a brand whisperer. You deserve to be compensated fairly for the value you bring to the table.

"The price of anything is the amount of life

you exchange for it." – Henry David Thoreau

This quote rings truer than ever in the digital marketing world. You're pouring your heart, soul, and countless hours into your work. Don't undervalue that effort by undercharging for your services.

Ditch the Bargaining Mindset

Imagine this: you walk into a fancy boutique, fall in love with a designer dress, and then proceed to haggle with the salesperson, begging them to slash the price in half. Sounds ridiculous, right? Yet, so many marketers fall into the trap of endless bargaining, undervaluing their services and eroding their profit margins.

Here's the thing: when you constantly negotiate your price, you're sending a clear message: "I'm not really sure I'm worth what I'm asking." This not only diminishes your perceived value but also attracts clients who are more interested in cheap deals than quality results.

The Confidence Equation

Confidence in your pricing stems from a deep understanding of your worth. Take the time to research industry standards, analyze your skills and experience, and factor in the value you bring to the table. Remember, you're not just selling services; you're selling solutions, expertise, and the potential for tangible results.

Setting Your Price: A No-Nonsense Approach

1. **Know Your Costs:** Calculate your overhead, expenses, and the time investment required for each project.

2. **Research Industry Standards:** Get a sense of what other marketers with similar experience and expertise are charging.

3. **Factor in Value:** Consider the unique value you bring to the table. Do you have specialized skills? A proven track record? These factors justify a premium price.

4. **Create Packages:** Offer tiered packages with varying levels of service and pricing to cater to different client budgets and needs.

5. **Communicate with Clarity:** Clearly outline your pricing structure and payment terms upfront to avoid confusion and ensure transparency.

The "No Discount" Dance

When a potential client tries to haggle, don't cave! Politely but firmly reiterate the value you offer and the reasons behind your pricing. If they're truly a good fit, they'll understand and appreciate your worth.

"It is not the creation of wealth that is wrong, but the love of money for its own sake." – Margaret Thatcher

This quote reminds us that while financial compensation is important, it shouldn't be the sole driving force behind your work. Focus on delivering exceptional results, building strong relationships with your clients, and making a genuine impact on their businesses. The financial rewards will follow.

Money-Back Guarantees: Proceed with Caution

While tempting, offering money-back guarantees can be a slippery slope, especially when you're starting out. Focus on delivering exceptional results and building a reputation for excellence. Your track record will speak for itself, attracting clients who value quality over empty promises.

Pricing your services confidently is a crucial step in building a successful and sustainable marketing agency. Remember, you're not just selling services; you're selling value, expertise, and the potential for transformative results. So ditch the bargaining mindset, embrace your worth, and confidently command the price you deserve.

Remember:

- **You are not a discount store.** You offer premium services that deserve premium pricing.

- **Your time is valuable.** Don't let clients dictate your schedule or demand unreasonable turnaround times.

- **Your well-being matters.** Take breaks, prioritize self-care, and avoid burnout.

By mastering the art of valuing your worth, you'll not only attract clients who respect your expertise but also create a business that is both financially rewarding and personally fulfilling. So

ditch the self-doubt, embrace your value,
and charge what you're worth.

Chapter 6: Show Up Like the Marketing Maestro You Are

Alright, my friend, you've mastered the art of referrals, built a killer network, and niched down like a boss. Now it's time to step into the spotlight and show the world what you're made of. This chapter is all about building a brand that screams "professionalism" and attracts clients like bees to honey.

Think of it this way: you're not just selling marketing services, you're selling yourself. Your image, your communication, and your online presence all play a crucial role in how potential clients perceive you.

Dress the Part (Yes, Even in Your Home Office)

"Dress for the job you want, not the job you have." This age-old adage holds true even in the digital age. While you might not need a three-piece suit for those Zoom calls, ditch the pajamas and opt for attire that says "I'm a serious business owner."

Why does this matter? Because how you present yourself influences how others perceive you. Dressing professionally boosts your confidence, commands respect, and signals to clients that you take your business seriously.

1. Social Media Stardom

- **Become a Platform Virtuoso:** LinkedIn, Instagram, Twitter (if that's still your jam)... master the platforms where your ideal clients hang out. Don't just create profiles, cultivate them. Share insightful content, engage in meaningful conversations, and showcase your personality.

- **Content is Your Currency:** Pump out high-quality content that positions you as a thought leader in your niche. Think insightful articles, eye-catching carousels, engaging Reels, and maybe even the occasional meme to show you're human (and have a sense of humor!).

- **Consistency is Key:** Social media isn't a one-night stand, It's a long-term relationship. Show up consistently, nurture your audience, and watch your online presence blossom.

Remember: *"Content is king, but engagement is queen and she rules the house!" – Gary Vaynerchuk*

2. Collaboration Nation

- **Partnerships = Power:** Don't be a lone wolf. Collaborate with other businesses, influencers, and even your competitors (gasp!). Guest blog, co-host webinars, participate in joint ventures – the possibilities are endless.

- **Expand Your Reach:** Collaboration exposes you to new audiences, amplifies your message, and builds valuable relationships. It's a win-win for everyone involved.

- **Cross-Promotion Power:** Leverage each other's platforms to promote your services and reach a wider audience. Think shoutouts, guest posts, and joint giveaways.

3. Professionalism: It's Not Just a Buzzword

- **Dress the Part:** Yes, even in the digital world, appearances matter. Ditch the pajamas and opt for attire that reflects the confident, successful marketer you are. (Pro tip: a blazer can do wonders for your Zoom meetings!)

- **Communication is Key:** Respond promptly to emails, be articulate in your communication, and always maintain a professional tone. Remember, you're representing your brand in every interaction.

- **Mind Your Manners:** Treat everyone with respect, even those who don't become clients. You never know who they might know or how your paths might cross in the future.

Remember: "Professionalism is not a label you give yourself – it's a description you hope others will apply to you.

4. Beyond the Surface

- **Continuous Learning:** The digital marketing landscape is constantly evolving. Stay ahead of the curve by investing in your professional development. Attend webinars, read industry publications, and never stop learning.
- **Embrace Feedback:** Don't be afraid to ask for feedback from clients, colleagues, and mentors. Constructive

criticism can help you identify areas for improvement and refine your approach.

- **Authenticity Wins:** Be yourself! Let your personality shine through in your interactions and your content. People connect with authenticity, so don't be afraid to show your true colors.

By mastering the art of showing up like a pro, you'll not only attract clients but also build a reputation for excellence that will serve you well for years to come. So ditch the sweatpants, embrace your inner marketing maestro, and get ready to shine!

Chapter 7: Seal the Deal (and Get Paid!) - Where Dreams Become Dollars

Congratulations, my friend! You've navigated the treacherous waters of client acquisition, charmed your prospects with your expertise, and now you're ready to reel them in. But hold on! Before you pop the champagne and start planning your victory dance, there's one crucial step left: sealing the deal and, most importantly, *getting paid*.

This chapter is your guide to navigating the final steps of the client-closing process, ensuring you get the respect, recognition, and remuneration you deserve.

The Invoice is King (or Queen!)

Remember this mantra: "A client isn't truly a client until they've paid." It's a harsh truth, but a necessary one. Don't fall into the trap of starting work before the invoice is settled. It's like building a house without a foundation – things can get messy, and you might end up with a pile of rubble (and unpaid invoices). Don't let this be you! Remember what Maya Angelou said: "Ask for what you want and be prepared to get it!"

Here's how to make invoicing a breeze:

- **Be Prompt:** Send your invoice as soon as the project scope and deliverables are finalized. Don't wait weeks or months; strike while the iron is hot.
- **Crystal Clear Clarity:** Your invoice should be a masterpiece of clarity. Clearly outline the services provided, the agreed-upon price, payment terms,

and deadlines. Leave no room for confusion or misinterpretation.

- **Embrace Technology:** Ditch the clunky spreadsheets and embrace invoicing software. Tools like Zoho Invoice, FreshBooks, or QuickBooks can automate the process, track payments, and even send automated reminders.

Secure Your Success: Contracts & Deliverables

Think of contracts and deliverables as your legal armor in the client-closing battlefield. They protect both you and your client, ensuring everyone is on the same page and minimizing the chances of misunderstandings or disputes.

- **Contracts: Your Safety Net:** A well-drafted contract is your legal safety net. It outlines the scope of work, payment terms, deadlines, and other crucial details. It also protects you from potential legal issues down the line.

- **Deliverables: Setting Expectations:** Clearly define the deliverables you'll be providing and the timeline for completion. This helps manage client expectations and ensures everyone is aligned on the project goals.

- **Communication is Key:** Discuss the contract and deliverables with your client in detail. Answer their questions, address their concerns, and ensure they fully understand the terms before signing on the dotted line.

Upfront Payment: Building Trust (and Securing Your Bag)

For recurring projects or long-term engagements, requesting a 50% upfront payment is a smart move. It not only secures your income but also builds trust with your client.

Think about it: when a client invests in your services upfront, they're demonstrating their commitment to the project and their confidence in your abilities. It's a win-win situation!

"Trust is the glue of life. It's the most essential ingredient in effective communication. It's the foundational principle that holds all relationships."

- Stephen Covey

Navigating the Payment Conversation

Discussing money can be awkward, but it's a crucial part of the client-closing process. Here's how to handle it like a pro:

- **Explain the rationale:** Clearly communicate to your client why you require an upfront payment. Explain that it allows you to dedicate resources to their project and ensures a smooth workflow.

- **Offer flexible payment options:** Provide various payment methods (e.g., bank transfer, online payment gateways) to make it convenient for your client.

- **Reassure them with transparency:** Provide regular updates and reports to keep your client informed about the progress of their project.

Celebrate the Wins (Big and Small)

Finally, don't forget to celebrate your successes! Landing a new client is a big deal, so take a moment to acknowledge your hard work and dedication. Whether it's a celebratory dance party, a fancy coffee treat, or simply a pat on the back, recognize your achievements and enjoy the fruits of your labor.

Remember, *"Success is not final, failure is not fatal: it is the courage to continue that counts." - Winston Churchill*

So go forth, my fellow marketers, armed with the knowledge and confidence to seal those deals and build a thriving agency. The world is waiting to be wowed by your marketing magic!

Okay, here are some extra bonus goodies to sprinkle throughout your "No Bluff, Just Super Stuff" guide:

Bonus Strategies & Examples:

- **The "Problem-Agitation-Solution" Framework:** This classic copywriting technique can be a powerful tool for client communication.
    - **Example:** "Struggling to get your website seen on Google? (Problem) It's frustrating to pour your heart into your business, only to be buried on page 10 of the search results. (Agitation) Let's optimize your website and get you ranking higher

so you can attract more customers. (Solution)"

- **The Power of "Social Proof":** Showcase testimonials, case studies, and success stories to build credibility and demonstrate your expertise.

    - **Example:** Include a section titled "Raving Fans" featuring glowing testimonials from satisfied clients.

- **Free Audits or Consultations:** Offer a free website audit, social media analysis, or marketing consultation as a lead magnet. This provides value upfront and positions you as an expert.

- **Example:** "Get a Free Website Audit and Discover Hidden Opportunities to Increase Your Leads!"

- **Content Marketing is Your Friend:** Create valuable blog posts, articles, or videos related to your niche. This establishes your authority and attracts potential clients.

  - **Example:** If you specialize in real estate marketing, write a blog post on "Top 10 Social Media Strategies for Real Estate Agents."

- **The "Foot-in-the-Door" Technique:** Start with a small, low-cost offer to get your foot in the door. Once you've proven your value, you can upsell higher-priced services.

    o **Example:** Offer a "Social Media Starter Package" that includes basic profile optimization and content creation.

- **Follow Up Like a Champ:** Don't give up after one attempt. Follow up with potential clients multiple times (without being annoying), providing additional value and demonstrating your persistence.

    o **Example:** After sending a proposal, follow up a few days later with a relevant industry article or case study.

- **Master the Art of Storytelling:** Use storytelling to connect with potential clients on an emotional level and make your services more relatable.

    - **Example:** Share a story about how you helped a struggling business achieve remarkable results through your marketing strategies.

- **Don't Underestimate the Power of a "Thank You":** Always express gratitude to potential clients for their time and consideration. A simple thank-you note can go a long way in building relationships.

Remember to weave these bonus strategies and examples throughout your guide to make it even more comprehensive and engaging for your readers.

Now Go Forth and Conquer!

So there you have it, my friend. The "No Bluff, Just Super Stuff" guide to conquering the client-closing game. Remember, this is a marathon, not a sprint. Building a successful agency takes time, effort, and a whole lot of hustle. But with the right strategies and a sprinkle of patience, you'll be well on your way to attracting dream clients and making a real impact in the digital marketing world.

Now, go forth and conquer! I believe in you. And remember, if you ever need a pep talk, a brainstorming buddy, or just someone to celebrate your wins with (because let's be honest, those wins deserve a happy dance!), I'm just a DM away.

Now, for your first mission:

1. **Share this guide:** Spread the client-closing love! Share this guide with your fellow marketers, friends, or anyone who might find it helpful. Let's build a community of empowered, successful digital marketers.

2. **Connect with me:** Let's connect on LinkedIn! I'd love to hear about your journey, your challenges, and your triumphs. Find me here: [Your LinkedIn Profile Link]

3. **Take action:** Don't just read this guide and let it gather digital dust. Put these strategies into action! Start reaching out, building your network, and crafting irresistible offers.

The world needs your marketing magic. Now go out there and make it happen!

www.ingramcontent.com/pod-product-compliance
Lightning Source LLC
Chambersburg PA
CBHW050320230526
45471CB00005B/2275